Scared to Lose You; Poems of Unspoken Love and Hidden Fears

Mrigendra Bharti

Published by Sellbrochure Vymish Entertainment, 2024.

SCARED TO LOSE YOU; POEMS OF UNSPOKEN LOVE AND HIDDEN FEARS

First edition. July 2, 2024.

Copyright © 2024 Mrigendra Bharti.

ISBN: 979-8227637901

Written by Mrigendra Bharti.

Table of Contents

Preface

Scared to Lose You: Poems of Unspoken Love and Hidden Fears
In the realm of human emotions, love stands as one of the most powerful and transformative forces. It has the ability to elevate us to unimaginable heights of joy and plunge us into the depths of despair. But amidst this whirlwind of emotions, there lies a quiet, often unspoken fear – the fear of losing the one we love.

This collection of poems delves into the heart of this fear, exploring the unspoken emotions and hidden anxieties that arise when love is threatened. Through the lens of a young man's unrequited love for his crush, we witness the delicate balance between hope and despair, the longing for connection and the fear of rejection.

The poems paint vivid portraits of stolen glances, fleeting moments of shared connection, and the gnawing ache of unreciprocated feelings. They capture the vulnerability of a heart laid bare, the fear of revealing one's true feelings, and the agonizing uncertainty of whether or not the love is returned.

As the poems unfold, we witness the protagonist's journey of self-discovery as he grapples with his fear of loss and the complexities of his own emotions. He learns to navigate the treacherous waters of unspoken love, confronting his fears and finding strength in his own vulnerability.

"Scared to Lose You" is a poignant and relatable collection that speaks to the universal human experience of love and loss. It is a testament to the power of words to capture the deepest emotions and to shed light on the hidden fears that often lie beneath the surface of our hearts.

Acknowledgment

In the tapestry of life, love weaves a thread of intricate emotions, painting our hearts with hues of joy, longing, and at times, the fear of loss. This collection of poems is a testament to this fear, a reflection of the unspoken love and hidden anxieties that arise when love feels threatened.

The inspiration for these verses lies in the depths of my own heart, where a flame of unspoken affection flickers, yearning for a spark to ignite it into a raging inferno. These poems are a tribute to the woman who has captured my heart, the one whose presence fills my world with a symphony of unspoken emotions.

I am deeply grateful to her for unknowingly stirring within me this whirlwind of emotions, for prompting me to explore the depths of my own vulnerability, and for reminding me of the power of love to both elevate and transform.

To my dear readers, I invite you to join me on this journey of self-discovery, as we navigate the treacherous waters of unspoken love, confronting our fears and finding strength in our own vulnerability. May these poems resonate with your own experiences, stirring within you a sense of empathy and understanding for the complexities of love and loss.

With a heart full of unspoken love and gratitude,
Mrigendra Bharti

About Sellbrochure Vymish Entertainment

Sellbrochure Vymish Entertainment, recognized as India's largest book publishing company, has made significant strides in ensuring its extensive collection of books reaches audiences across the global market. This rapid expansion is a testament to the company's dedication to disseminating knowledge and literature far beyond national borders. Central to its success is its affiliation with InkWhirl Media Networks, a reputable entity in the media and publication industry known for its innovative and strategic approaches. Within this network, InkWhirl Publication LLC operates as a vital division, further enhancing the company's capabilities and reach in the international market. The visionary behind this enterprise is Mrigendra Bharti, the founder of Sellbrochure Vymish Entertainment. His foresight and passion for the literary world have been instrumental in steering the company towards remarkable growth and recognition. Under his leadership, Sellbrochure Vymish Entertainment has not only expanded its catalog but also established a strong presence in both domestic and international markets. Mrigendra Bharti's commitment to excellence and innovation has been a driving force in the company's journey, ensuring that it stays ahead of industry trends and meets the evolving needs of readers worldwide.

Sellbrochure Vymish Entertainment operates under the robust support of its parental organization, Mrigendra Bharti Group InfoTech. This affiliation provides the necessary resources and strategic guidance, enabling the publishing company to undertake ambitious projects and explore new markets. Mrigendra Bharti Group InfoTech's extensive experience in technology and information services has been a valuable asset, allowing Sellbrochure Vymish Entertainment to integrate advanced digital solutions in its operations, thereby enhancing its distribution capabilities and reader engagement.

Through relentless efforts and a commitment to quality, Sellbrochure Vymish Entertainment continues to break barriers and expand the reach of Indian literature globally. The company's diverse portfolio includes a wide range of genres, catering to different age groups and interests, thereby fostering a rich and inclusive reading culture. As it continues to innovate and grow, Sellbrochure Vymish Entertainment remains dedicated to its mission of making literature accessible to all, contributing significantly to the global literary landscape.

Connect With Mrigendra,
Thank you very much for choosing this book.
You can also connect with me on Instagram,
https://www.instagram.com/i_mrigendrabharti.official
With Love,
Mrigendra Bharti

Introduction

Have you ever found yourself captivated by someone, their very presence igniting a symphony of unspoken emotions within you? A silent movie plays behind your eyelids, a story woven with stolen glances, fleeting moments of connection, and the gnawing ache of unrequited feelings. This collection of poems, "Scared to Lose You," delves into the heart of this experience, exploring the hidden anxieties and vulnerabilities that arise when love feels threatened.

Imagine yourself a young man, captivated by a girl. Her laughter echoes through the library, a melody that disrupts the studious silence and sets your heart racing. But between you lies a chasm of unspoken words and unspoken fears. You fear that your love might forever remain a flickering flame, lost in the vast ocean of time.

These poems are a testament to this struggle. They are the whispers of a love yet to be confessed, a tapestry of yearning and uncertainty. Each verse paints a vivid portrait of stolen glances, shy smiles, and the bittersweet ache of unrequited affection.

As you turn the pages, prepare to enter the sanctuary of a love-stricken heart. Here, hope battles fear, and longing wrestles with the constant dread of losing what you hold dear.

These verses are a testament to the silent language of the heart, a language spoken in stolen glances, shy smiles, and the bittersweet ache of unspoken love.

"Scared to Lose You" is an invitation to delve into the depths of unspoken affection, a journey where fear and hope dance a precarious tango. It's a poignant exploration of the universal human experience of love, loss, and the courage it takes to confront our deepest fears.

Unfulfilled Melody

In the depths of my heart, a flame does reside,
For you, my love, my heart's true guide.
Your smile, a sunbeam, warm and bright,
Your eyes, like stars, twinkling in the night.
Oh, don't leave me yet, my darling dear,
My heart is still full, my love is clear.
Like a bird without wings, I'd lose my way,
If you were to vanish, leaving me in dismay.
Your presence, a balm, soothing my soul,
Your touch, a whisper, making me whole.
In the tapestry of my life, you're the golden thread,
Without you, my dear, my dreams are dead.
So stay with me, my love, my heart's desire,
Let our love burn with an eternal fire.
Together we'll face whatever life may bring,
Two souls entwined, forever we'll sing.

Lingering Moonlight

As the moon casts its glow on the silent night,
My heart yearns for you, with all its might.
Your absence echoes, a haunting refrain,
A melody of sorrow, causing me pain.
Oh, don't leave me yet, my love so true,
My heart is still heavy, with longing for you.
Like a flower without rain, I'd wilt and fade,
If you were to depart, leaving me in shade.
Your voice, a symphony, sweet and serene,
Your laughter, a melody, like a joyful scene.
In the garden of my life, you're the blooming rose,
Without you, my dear, my happiness goes.
So stay with me, my love, my heart's delight,
Let our love blossom, shining ever so bright.
Together we'll dance under the starry sky,
Two hearts united, soaring ever so high.

Starlight's Embrace

In the depths of my thoughts, your image resides,
A vision of beauty, where my heart confides.
Your smile, a sunrise, chasing away the night,
Your eyes, like oceans, deep and full of light.
Oh, don't leave me yet, my love so dear,
My heart is still yearning, my love is clear.
Like a boat without sails, I'd drift and sway,
If you were to vanish, leaving me astray.
Your presence, a haven, where I find my peace,
Your touch, a magic spell, making sorrows cease.
In the tapestry of my dreams, you're the guiding star,
Without you, my dear, I'd be lost afar.
So stay with me, my love, my heart's desire,
Let our love blossom, burning with eternal fire.
Together we'll face whatever life may bring,
Two souls entwined, forever we'll sing.

Whispers in the Wind

As the breeze whispers through the rustling leaves,
My heart whispers your name, it truly believes.
Your smile, a rainbow, painting my world with hue,
Your eyes, like galaxies, filled with dreams I pursue.
Oh, don't leave me yet, my love so true,
My heart is still heavy, with longing for you.
Like a bird without wings, I'd lose my way,
If you were to vanish, leaving me in dismay.
Your voice, a melody, enchanting my soul,
Your laughter, a symphony, making my spirit whole.
In the garden of life, you're the blooming rose,
Without you, my dear, my happiness goes.
So stay with me, my love, my heart's delight,
Let our love blossom, shining ever so bright.
Together we'll dance under the starry sky,
Two hearts united, soaring ever so high.

Yearning for Sunshine

In the depths of my being, your love resides,
A flame that flickers, where my hope confides.
Your smile, a sunshine, warming my soul,
Your eyes, like stars, making my spirit whole.
Oh, don't leave me yet, my love so dear,
My heart is still yearning, my love is clear.
Like a tree without roots, I'd wither and fade,
If you were to depart, leaving me in shade.
Your presence, a comfort, where I find my rest,
Your touch, a gentle breeze, soothing my breast.
In the tapestry of my dreams, you're the golden thread,
Without you, my dear, my joy is dead.

Unwavering Devotion

In the depths of my heart, your love resides,
A flame that burns, where my soul confides.
Your smile, a sunrise, chasing away the night,
Your eyes, like stars, illuminating my sight.
Oh, don't leave me yet, my love so true,
My heart is still full, my love for you grew.
Like a bird without wings, I'd lose my way,
If you were to vanish, leaving me in dismay.
Your presence, a haven, where I find my peace,
Your touch, a gentle breeze, making my sorrows cease.
In the tapestry of my life, you're the golden thread,
Without you, my dear, my dreams are dead.
So stay with me, my love, my heart's desire,
Let our love blossom, burning with eternal fire.
Together we'll face whatever life may bring,
Two souls entwined, forever we'll sing.

Eternal Bond

As the moon casts its glow on the silent night,
My heart yearns for you, with all its might.
Your absence echoes, a haunting refrain,
A melody of sorrow, causing me pain.
Oh, don't leave me yet, my love so dear,
My heart is still heavy, with longing for you, my dear.
Like a flower without rain, I'd wilt and fade,
If you were to depart, leaving me in shade.
Your voice, a symphony, sweet and serene,
Your laughter, a melody, like a joyful scene.
In the garden of my life, you're the blooming rose,
Without you, my dear, my happiness goes.
So stay with me, my love, my heart's delight,
Let our love blossom, shining ever so bright.
Together we'll dance under the starry sky,
Two hearts united, soaring ever so high.

Inseparable Souls

In the depths of my thoughts, your image resides,
A vision of beauty, where my heart confides.
Your smile, a sunrise, chasing away the night,
Your eyes, like oceans, deep and full of light.
Oh, don't leave me yet, my love so true,
My heart is still yearning, my love for you grew.
Like a boat without sails, I'd drift and sway,
If you were to vanish, leaving me astray.
Your presence, a haven, where I find my peace,
Your touch, a magic spell, making sorrows cease.
In the tapestry of my dreams, you're the guiding star,
Without you, my dear, I'd be lost afar.
So stay with me, my love, my heart's desire,
Let our love blossom, burning with eternal fire.
Together we'll face whatever life may bring,
Two souls entwined, forever we'll sing.

Enduring Love

As the breeze whispers through the rustling leaves,
My heart whispers your name, it truly believes.
Your smile, a rainbow, painting my world with hue,
Your eyes, like galaxies, filled with dreams I pursue.
Oh, don't leave me yet, my love so true,
My heart is still heavy, with longing for you.
Like a bird without wings, I'd lose my way,
If you were to vanish, leaving me in dismay.
Your voice, a melody, enchanting my soul,
Your laughter, a symphony, making my spirit whole.
In the garden of life, you're the blooming rose,
Without you, my dear, my happiness goes.
So stay with me, my love, my heart's delight,
Let our love blossom, shining ever so bright.
Together we'll dance under the starry sky,
Two hearts united, soaring ever so high.

Silent Symphony

The world fades silent when you're by my side,
A symphony of emotions, deep inside.
Your smile, a melody that makes my heart sing,
Your eyes, a captivating poem, taking wing.
Don't leave just yet, my love, my sweetest sound,
My heart's symphony for you is unbound.
Like a song without rhythm, I'd fall incomplete,
If your presence faded, leaving a silent beat.
Your laughter, a harmony, chasing away despair,
Your touch, a soothing note, a gentle prayer.
In the orchestra of my life, you're the conductor's grace,
Without you, my dear, my music would erase.
So stay with me, my love, my heart's maestro,
Let our love's symphony play, forever grow.
Together we'll compose a beautiful refrain,
Two souls entwined, in a love's sweet domain.

Fear of Falling

The depths of my heart, for you they yearn,
A love that blossoms, a passion that burns.
Your smile, a sunrise, warm on my face,
Your eyes, a galaxy, a mesmerizing space.
Oh, don't leave me yet, my love, don't stray,
The thought of losing you, takes my breath away.
Like a climber without a rope, I'd surely fall,
If you were to vanish, leaving an empty wall.
Your presence, a comfort, a grounding force,
Your touch, a safe harbor, on a stormy course.
In the journey of my life, you're the guiding light,
Without you, my dear, I'd lose my sight.
So stay with me, my love, my hand to hold,
Let our love grow stronger, a story untold.
Together we'll face the mountains we may climb,
Two souls connected, through all of time.

Whispers of the Heart

In the hush of twilight, whispers take flight,
Words of affection, beneath the starry night.
Your smile, a moonbeam, casting a gentle glow,
Your eyes, a universe, where my feelings flow.
Oh, don't leave me yet, my love, my silent plea,
The thought of your absence, fills me with misery.
Like a seedling without sunshine, I'd fail to grow,
If your presence faded, leaving a heart of woe.
Your voice, a soothing balm, calming my fears,
Your laughter, a vibrant song, erasing all tears.
In the garden of my life, you're the blossoming bloom,
Without you, my dear, my world is consumed.
So stay with me, my love, the whisperer of dreams,
Let our love flourish, like a cascading stream.
Together we'll paint a future, vibrant and bright,
Two souls intertwined, bathed in love's light.

Colors of My World

The world was muted, a canvas in gray,
Until you arrived, and chased the blues away.
Your smile, a burst of color, painting the skies,
Your eyes, sparkling jewels, reflecting sunrise.
Oh, don't leave me yet, my love, my vibrant hue,
The thought of a world without you, is a lonely view.
Like a painter without a brush, I'd lose my art,
If your presence faded, tearing my world apart.
Your voice, a melody, that fills the air,
Your touch, a masterpiece, a love beyond compare.
In the tapestry of my life, you're the vibrant thread,
Without you, my dear, my colors would shed.
So stay with me, my love, my muse and desire,
Let our love be a masterpiece, set the world on fire.
Together we'll create a life, colorful and bold,
Two souls united, a story to be told.

The Language of Love

Words seem to falter, when you're near,
My heart speaks volumes, though my voice unclear.
Your smile, a poem, written in grace,
Your eyes, a story, etched on my face.
Don't leave yet, my love, let our connection grow,
This language unspoken, my heart longs to know.
Like a writer without words, my thoughts would fade,
If your presence vanished, leaving a void unmade.
Your laughter, a melody, my spirit takes flight,
Your touch, a whisper, a starlit night.
In the library of my life, you're the wisdom I seek,
Without you, my dear, my knowledge would be weak.
So stay with me, my love, my muse and desire,
Let our love blossom, a story set afire.
Together we'll translate the whispers of the heart,
Two souls entwined, a love-filled work of art.

Destiny's Embrace

The stars have aligned, our paths they did meet,
Two souls connected, a love bittersweet.
Your smile, a compass, guiding me true,
Your eyes, a galaxy, where dreams come anew.
Don't leave yet, my love, destiny's hand,
Has brought us together, in this love-struck land.
Like a ship without a sail, I'd drift on the tide,
If your presence faded, lost without a guide.
Your voice, a siren's song, luring me near,
Your touch, a safe harbor, casting away fear.
In the tapestry of fate, you're the thread of gold,
Without you, my dear, my story untold.
So stay with me, my love, destiny's embrace,
Let our love flourish, leaving an everlasting trace.
Together we'll sail the currents of life's unknown sea,
Two souls intertwined, eternally free.

A Spark of Forever

A spark ignited, the moment we met,
A flame that burns brighter, with every sunset.
Your smile, a wildfire, consuming all doubt,
Your eyes, a galaxy, where love's wonders sprout.
Don't leave yet, my love, the embers still glow,
This spark of forever, only you can know.
Like a fire without fuel, I'd dwindle and cease,
If your presence faded, leaving a heart-aching peace.
Your voice, a crackling warmth, chasing away cold,
Your touch, a gentle heat, a story yet untold.
In the hearth of my life, you're the burning flame,
Without you, my dear, my passion would be tame.
So stay with me, my love, the keeper of the spark,
Let our love blaze brightly, leaving its mark.
Together we'll ignite a fire, forever to burn,
Two souls intertwined, a love that will learn.

Symphony of Our Souls

A silent melody plays, when you're by my side,
A symphony of emotions, that our hearts confide.
Your smile, the sweetest note, a harmonious blend,
Your eyes, a captivating verse, that knows no end.
Don't leave yet, my love, the music's incomplete,
This symphony of our souls, so divinely sweet.
Like a conductor without an orchestra, I'd lose my way,
If your presence faded, the music would stray.
Your laughter, a crescendo, lifting my spirits high,
Your touch, a calming note, a teardrop's soft sigh.
In the grand performance of life, you're the maestro's grace,
Without you, my dear, the music would erase.
So stay with me, my love, and compose our refrain,
Let our love's symphony forever remain.
Together we'll create a masterpiece untold,
Two souls entwined, a love story to behold.

Captivated by Your Light

The moon pales in comparison, when your smile ignites,
A radiant glow that banishes the darkest nights.
Your eyes, like twin stars, hold a celestial gleam,
A universe of wonder, captured in a dream.
Don't leave yet, my love, let your brilliance shine,
In your presence, a magic, truly divine.
Like a sunflower without the sun, I'd wilt and droop,
If your light extinguished, leaving me in a loop.
Your laughter, a melody, that sets my soul alight,
Your touch, a gentle current, guiding me through the night.
In the vast expanse of my life, you're the guiding star,
Without you, my dear, I'd wander lost and far.
So stay with me, my love, my beacon in the storm,
Let our love illuminate the path, keeping us warm.
Together we'll chase the shadows and embrace the day,
Two souls entwined, forever bathed in love's ray.

Entangled Destinies

Our fates intertwined, like branches of a tree,
Destined to grow together, eternally.
Your smile, a summer breeze, whispering secrets true,
Your eyes, a captivating ocean, with depths of endless blue.
Don't leave yet, my love, our story's just begun,
This tapestry of destiny, forever to be spun.
Like a vine without a trellis, I'd fall and break,
If your presence faded, leaving a heart's ache.
Your voice, a soothing murmur, calming every fear,
Your touch, a grounding root, keeping me ever near.
In the garden of life, you're the bloom beside mine,
Without you, my dear, my purpose would decline.
So stay with me, my love, our destinies entwined,
Let our love blossom, a love forever enshrined.
Together we'll weather the storms, and bask in the sun,
Two souls connected, as one.

Aching Silence in Your Absence

The world falls silent, when you're not here,
An emptiness echoes, a loneliness I fear.
Your smile, a vibrant song, that fills the air,
Your eyes, a captivating story, beyond compare.
Don't leave yet, my love, let your presence remain,
This deafening silence, drives me insane.
Like a bird without a song, I'd lose my voice,
If your presence faded, leaving a heart with no choice.
Your laughter, a melody, that chases away despair,
Your touch, a whispered promise, a love beyond compare.
In the symphony of my life, you're the sweetest note,
Without you, my dear, my music would float, lost and remote.
So stay with me, my love, and fill the void with sound,
Let our love's symphony forever resound.
Together we'll create a harmony, vibrant and true,
Two souls entwined, me and you.

A Compass to My Heart

Lost in a world unknown, before you I met,
A wandering soul, with a love unkept.
Your smile, a guiding light, through the darkest maze,
Your eyes, a map to my heart, dispelling all haze.
Don't leave yet, my love, be my compass so true,
Lead me on this journey, with a love ever new.
Like a sailor without a star, I'd be lost at sea,
If your presence faded, leaving no part of me.
Your voice, a soothing current, guiding me to shore,
Your touch, a safe harbor, wanting nothing more.
In the vast ocean of life, you're the steady breeze,
Without you, my dear, I'd drift beyond the seas.
So stay with me, my love, and navigate my way,
Let our love be the anchor, forever here to stay.
Together we'll explore uncharted territory, hand in hand,
Two souls entwined, forever in this love-struck land.

Captured in Your Constellation

Amongst the vast expanse of faces I see,
Only yours ignites a spark within me.
Your smile, a constellation, dazzling and bright,
Your eyes, galaxies swirling, with a captivating light.
Don't leave yet, my love, let me get lost in your gleam,
In your presence, a magic, a fantastical dream.
Like a star without a sky, I'd lose my shine,
If your light extinguished, leaving a heart that's not thine.
Your laughter, a cosmic melody, filling the void,
Your touch, a shooting star, a wish deployed.
In the universe of my life, you're the stardust I crave,
Without you, my dear, I'd be forever enslaved to the grave.
So stay with me, my love, my celestial guide,
Let our love form a nebula, where emotions confide.
Together we'll explore the universe's unknown way,
Two souls entwined, forever basking in love's soft ray.

A Timeless Melody

The rhythm of my heart beats only for you,
A timeless melody, forever ringing true.
Your smile, a harmonious note, played with gentle grace,
Your eyes, a captivating verse, etched upon my face.
Don't leave yet, my love, the music lingers on,
This symphony of our souls, a love that carries on.
Like a song unheard, my emotions would fade,
If your presence faded, leaving a sorrowful cascade.
Your laughter, a joyful chorus, uplifting my spirit high,
Your touch, a calming bridge, where tears softly lie.
In the grand orchestra of life, you're the maestro's delight,
Without you, my dear, my music would lose its light.
So stay with me, my love, and conduct our refrain,
Let our love's symphony forever entertain.
Together we'll compose a timeless masterpiece untold,
Two souls entwined, a love story to unfold.

Where Words Fail, My Heart Speaks

When words stumble and falter, in your presence I stand,
My heart speaks volumes, emotions out of hand.
Your smile, a poem whispered, on a gentle summer breeze,
Your eyes, a story painted, for only me to appease.
Don't leave yet, my love, let our connection grow,
This language unspoken, a depth only hearts can know.
Like a writer without ink, my thoughts would take flight,
If your presence faded, leaving an everlasting night.
Your laughter, a vibrant sonnet, sets my soul ablaze,
Your touch, an unwritten chapter, turning life's winding maze.
In the library of my life, you're the wisdom I hold dear,
Without you, my love, my knowledge incomplete, I fear.
So stay with me, my love, my muse and my desire,
Let our love blossom, a story set on fire.
Together we'll translate the whispers of the heart,
Two souls entwined, a love-filled work of art.

A Tapestry Woven with Love

Thread by thread, our connection we weave,
A tapestry of love, for our hearts to believe.
Your smile, a vibrant hue, adding warmth to the design,
Your eyes, a depth of emotion, where love's essence entwine.
Don't leave yet, my love, let's continue to create,
This tapestry of our journey, defying fate.
Like a loom without a weaver, the threads would unwind,
If your presence faded, leaving my story left behind.
Your laughter, a shimmering thread, woven with glee,
Your touch, a comforting thread, setting my spirit free.
In the grand design of life, you're the pattern I adore,
Without you, my dear, my masterpiece would be no more.
So stay with me, my love, and let's weave hand in hand,
Let our love's tapestry forever withstand.
Together we'll create a masterpiece, vibrant and bold,
Two souls entwined, a story forever to be told.

A Dream Painted in Your Eyes

The world I knew fades, when I gaze in your eyes,
A dream unfolds, painted with vibrant skies.
Your smile, a sunrise, chasing away the night,
Your eyes, a captivating ocean, reflecting endless light.
Don't leave yet, my love, let the dream remain,
This world we create, eases every pain.
Like an artist without a brush, my vision would blur,
If your presence faded, leaving my canvas stir.
Your laughter, a gentle melody, calming the storm,
Your touch, a whispered promise, keeping me warm.
In the gallery of my life, you're the masterpiece I see,
Without you, my dear, my art would cease to be.
So stay with me, my love, and paint our world anew,
Let our love's masterpiece forever come true.
Together we'll create a vibrant story untold,
Two souls entwined, in a love forever bold.

A Whisper Carried on the Wind

A silent whisper escapes my lips, your name it carries,
On the gentle breeze, across the valleys and prairies.
Your smile, a blooming flower, fragrant and sweet,
Your eyes, a starlit sky, where dreams and hopes meet.
Don't leave yet, my love, let the whisper be heard,
This silent yearning, a love unspoken, a precious word.
Like a seed without rain, my feelings would wither and fade,
If your presence faded, leaving a love unmade.
Your laughter, a cascading waterfall, pure and bright,
Your touch, a gentle sigh, chasing away the night.
In the garden of my life, you're the bloom I hold dear,
Without you, my dear, my happiness disappears.
So stay with me, my love, and let the whisper take flight,
Let our love blossom, bathed in love's gentle light.
Together we'll grow a love story, strong and true,
Two souls entwined, me and you.

A Melody Composed for You

A symphony plays within my heart, a melody all for you,
A crescendo of emotions, forever honest and true.
Your smile, the sweetest note, a harmony so bright,
Your eyes, a captivating verse, filling my world with light.
Don't leave yet, my love, let the music flow,
This symphony of our souls, where love's embers glow.
Like a musician without a song, I'd lose my voice,
If your presence faded, leaving only a hollow choice.
Your laughter, a vibrant chorus, lifting my spirit high,
Your touch, a calming bridge, where tears softly lie.
In the grand orchestra of life, you're the conductor's grace,
Without you, my dear, my music would lose its embrace.
So stay with me, my love, and compose with me,
Let our love's symphony forever set us free.
Together we'll create a masterpiece, vibrant and bold,
Two souls entwined, a love story to be told.

A Haven in Your Presence

The world may rage on, with chaos and strife,
But in your presence, I find solace in life.
Your smile, a calming sunset, painting the sky with ease,
Your eyes, a tranquil ocean, bringing me inner peace.
Don't leave yet, my love, be my haven and guide,
A shelter from storms, where love can reside.
Like a lost soul without a home, I'd wander astray,
If your presence faded, leaving my heart in disarray.
Your laughter, a soothing current, washing worries away,
Your touch, a safe harbor, where I can forever stay.
In the journey of life, you're the lighthouse I see,
Without you, my dear, I'd be lost at sea.
So stay with me, my love, be my haven so true,
Let our love be a fortress, forever me and you.
Together we'll face the storms, hand in hand, side by side,
Two souls entwined, in love's everlasting tide.

A Butterfly Drawn to Your Light

A fluttering butterfly, my heart takes flight,
Drawn to your warmth, a radiant guiding light.
Your smile, a sunbeam, chasing away the gray,
Your eyes, a vibrant garden, where dreams come to play.
Don't leave yet, my love, let me bask in your glow,
This magnetic pull, a love destined to grow.
Like a butterfly without a flower, I'd lose my way,
If your presence faded, leaving a heart in dismay.
Your laughter, a melody of joy, that sets my spirit free,
Your touch, a gentle breeze, whispering promises to me.
In the meadow of my life, you're the bloom I adore,
Without you, my dear, my colors would fade evermore.
So stay with me, my love, and let our wings unfurl,
Let our love blossom, a love for all the world.
Together we'll dance on the wind, a vibrant display,
Two souls entwined, forever soaring away.

A Spark That Ignites the Soul

A spark ignites, the moment you appear,
A warmth within my soul, banishing all my fear.
Your smile, a crackling fire, igniting all I hold dear,
Your eyes, a mesmerizing flame, where love and wonder are clear.
Don't leave yet, my love, let the spark ignite,
This burning passion, a love forever bright.
Like a hearth without embers, my spirit would grow cold,
If your presence faded, leaving a story untold.
Your laughter, a crackling warmth, chases away the chill,
Your touch, a gentle ember, setting my heart athrill.
In the fireplace of my life, you're the flame I hold near,
Without you, my dear, my warmth would disappear.
So stay with me, my love, and keep the fire alive,
Let our love's embers forever burn and thrive.
Together we'll create a warmth, to chase away the night,
Two souls entwined, bathed in love's radiant light.

A Story Written in the Stars

Our destinies intertwined, written in the stars above,
A story unfolding, a testament to endless love.
Your smile, a constellation, guiding me through the night,
Your eyes, a captivating galaxy, filled with endless light.
Don't leave yet, my love, let the story unfold,
This celestial connection, more precious than gold.
Like a lost traveler without a map, I'd wander astray,
If your presence faded, leaving me lost in the way.
Your laughter, a cosmic melody, filling the universe with glee,
Your touch, a shooting star, a wish whispered for me.
In the vast expanse of life, you're the gravity I crave,
Without you, my dear, I'd be forever adrift and enslaved.
So stay with me, my love, and navigate by my side,
Let our love's story forever be our guide.
Together we'll explore the cosmos, hand in hand,
Two souls entwined, forever in this love-struck land.

A Rhythm That Beats for You

A steady rhythm beats within my chest,
A melody of love, forever putting me to the test.
Your smile, the sweetest harmony, a song I long to hear,
Your eyes, a captivating verse, forever drawing me near.
Don't leave yet, my love, let the rhythm flow,
This symphony of our souls, a love meant to grow.
Like a drummer without a beat, my heart would lose its sound,
If your presence faded, leaving a silence profound.
Your laughter, a vibrant chorus, that sets my spirit free,
Your touch, a calming bridge, where tears softly flee.
In the grand orchestra of life, you're the conductor's delight,
Without you, my dear, my music would lose its light.
So stay with me, my love, and compose with me hand in hand,
Let our love's symphony forever take a stand.
Together we'll create a masterpiece, vibrant and bold,
Two souls entwined, a story forever to be told.

The Language of a Glance

Words may escape me, tongue tied and shy,
But a glance in your eyes speaks volumes that fly.
Your smile, a secret whispered, on a summer breeze,
Your eyes, a captivating story, that puts my heart at ease.
Don't leave yet, my love, let our connection grow,
This language unspoken, a depth only hearts can know.
Like a writer without a pen, my thoughts would take flight,
If your presence faded, leaving an everlasting night.
Your laughter, a vibrant sonnet, sets my soul ablaze,
Your touch, an unwritten chapter, turning life's winding maze.
In the library of my life, you're the wisdom I seek,
Without you, my dear, my knowledge would be weak.
So stay with me, my love, the interpreter of my heart,
Let our love blossom, a love story set to restart.
Together we'll translate the whispers unspoken and true,
Two souls entwined, in a love forever new.

A Compass Lost at Sea

A sailor adrift, on a vast, lonely sea,
Without you, my compass, I'd be forever lost, you see.
Your smile, a guiding lighthouse, piercing the darkest night,
Your eyes, a captivating ocean, reflecting endless light.
Don't leave yet, my love, be my anchor and guide,
A steady presence, in whom my heart can confide.
Like a ship without a sail, I'd drift on the tide,
If your presence faded, leaving nowhere to hide.
Your laughter, a soothing current, calming the storm,
Your touch, a safe harbor, keeping me warm.
In the vast ocean of life, you're the steady breeze,
Without you, my dear, I'd drift beyond the seas.
So stay with me, my love, navigate me to shore,
Let our love be the anchor, forevermore.
Together we'll explore uncharted territory, side by side,
Two souls entwined, forever in love's ocean to confide.

A Melody Composed in Silence

A silent melody plays within my soul,
A symphony of emotions, waiting to take control.
Your smile, the sweetest note, a harmony so bright,
Your eyes, a captivating verse, filling my world with light.
Don't leave yet, my love, let the music flow,
This symphony unspoken, a love destined to grow.
Like a musician without an instrument, my voice would be weak,
If your presence faded, leaving a melody incomplete.
Your laughter, a vibrant song, that sets my spirit free,
Your touch, a calming bridge, where worries cease to be.
In the grand orchestra of life, you're the conductor's grace,
Without you, my dear, my music would lose its embrace.
So stay with me, my love, and compose with me in the hush,
Let our love's symphony forever create a rush.
Together we'll create a masterpiece, vibrant and untold,
Two souls entwined, in a love story to unfold.

A Tapestry Woven with Laughter

Thread by thread, our connection we weave,
A tapestry of laughter, for our hearts to believe.
Your smile, a vibrant hue, adding joy to the design,
Your eyes, a depth of emotion, where happiness intertwine.
Don't leave yet, my love, let the laughter remain,
This tapestry of our journey, eases every pain.
Like a loom without a weaver, the threads would unwind,
If your presence faded, leaving my story left behind.
Your laughter, a shimmering thread, woven with glee,
Your touch, a comforting thread, setting my spirit free.
In the grand design of life, you're the pattern I adore,
Without you, my dear, my world would be dull once more.
So stay with me, my love, and let's weave hand in hand,
Let our love's tapestry forever withstand.
Together we'll create a masterpiece, vibrant and bright,
Two souls entwined, bathed in love's laughter and light.

A Whisper Carried on the Wind (A Different Take)

The wind whispers your name, a secret it carries along,
Through rustling leaves and swaying grass, a love forever strong.
Your smile, a gentle breeze, caressing my face with delight,
Your eyes, a calm meadow, where dreams take flight.
Don't leave yet, my love, let the whispers linger near,
This melody of affection, erasing every fear.
Like a wilting flower without sunlight's embrace,
If your presence faded, leaving an empty space.
Your laughter, a cascading stream, pure and ever bright,
Your touch, a field of wildflowers, blooming in the morning light.
In the garden of my life, you're the bloom I hold most dear,
Without you, my love, my happiness would disappear.
So stay with me, my love, let the whispers unfold,
Let our love blossom, a story yet to be told.
Together we'll grow a love story, strong and true,
Two souls entwined, forever bathed in love's morning dew.

A Constellation of Feelings

A million stars ignite, when you enter the scene,
A constellation of feelings, a love that's ever keen.
Your smile, a supernova, exploding with radiant glee,
Your eyes, celestial bodies, where wonder I can see.
Don't leave yet, my love, let the stars shine so bright,
This cosmic connection, a love that burns ever so light.
Like a lost astronaut without a ship to guide,
If your presence faded, nowhere for me to hide.
Your laughter, a shooting star, a wish whispered in the night,
Your touch, the gentle pull of gravity, holding me ever so tight.
In the vast universe of life, you're the galaxy I crave,
Without you, my dear, I'd be forever lost and enslaved.
So stay with me, my love, navigate the celestial way,
Let our love's constellation forever light our day.
Together we'll explore the cosmos, hand in hand, you and I,
Two souls entwined, beneath love's endless sky.

A Story Written in Laughter

Laughter lines etched upon my face, a testament to you,
A story written in joy, forever honest and true.
Your smile, the punchline to a joke, a burst of delight,
Your eyes, a captivating story, sparkling ever so bright.
Don't leave yet, my love, let the laughter remain,
This symphony of our souls, a love that eases all pain.
Like a comedian without an audience, my jokes would fall flat,
If your presence faded, leaving my humor to splatter and splat.
Your laughter, a contagious melody, uplifting my spirit so high,
Your touch, a shared punchline, a silent tear in my eye.
In the grand theater of life, you're the spotlight I adore,
Without you, my dear, my performance would be an endless chore.
So stay with me, my love, and laugh with me hand in hand,
Let our love's story be a masterpiece, forever withstand.
Together we'll create a joyful performance, vibrant and bold,
Two souls entwined, a love story forever to be told.

A Haven in Your Smile

The world may rage on, with its chaos and strife,
But within your smile, I find solace in life.
Your smile, a calming sunset, painting the sky with ease,
Your eyes, a tranquil ocean, bringing me inner peace.
Don't leave yet, my love, be my haven and guide,
A shelter from storms, where love can confide.
Like a trembling flame without a candle's embrace,
If your presence faded, leaving an empty space.
Your laughter, a soothing current, washing worries away,
Your touch, a safe harbor, where I can forever stay.
In the journey of life, you're the lighthouse I see,
Without you, my dear, I'd be lost at sea.
So stay with me, my love, and let your smile always shine,
Let our love be a fortress, forever entwined.
Together we'll face the storms, a team, strong and true,
Two souls entwined, in love's everlasting hue.

A Symphony of Colors

The world turns grayscale, when you're not in sight,
But with you, my love, colors burst ever so bright.
Your smile, a vibrant palette, a masterpiece untold,
Your eyes, a captivating canvas, with stories to unfold.
Don't leave yet, my love, let the colors remain,
This vibrant tapestry, a love that eases all pain.
Like an artist without a brush, my world would lose its hue,
If your presence faded, leaving a colorless view.
Your laughter, a melody of joy, painting the sky with glee,
Your touch, a gentle whisper, a color whispered to me.
In the gallery of my life, you're the masterpiece I adore,
Without you, my dear, my world would be dull once more.
So stay with me, my love, and paint our world anew,
Let our love's masterpiece forever come true.
Together we'll create a vibrant story, bold and bright,
Two souls entwined, bathed in love's eternal light.

A Secret Language in Your Touch

Words fail me utterly, when your hand meets mine,
A secret language spoken, a love that's truly divine.
Your smile, a whispered promise, on a gentle summer breeze,
Your eyes, a captivating story, that puts my heart at ease.
Don't leave yet, my love, let the connection grow,
This unspoken language, a depth only hearts can know.
Like a dancer without a partner, my steps would lose their grace,
If your presence faded, leaving an empty space.
Your laughter, a vibrant chorus, that sets my spirit free,
Your touch, a calming bridge, where tears softly flee.
In the grand dance of life, you're the partner I hold near,
Without you, my dear, my steps would falter, filled with fear.
So stay with me, my love, and dance with me hand in hand,
Let our love's language forever take a stand.
Together we'll create a masterpiece, vibrant and bold,
Two souls entwined, a story forever to be told.

A Spark That Ignites the Mind

A spark ignites within, the moment you appear,
A curiosity awakened, a love both sweet and clear.
Your smile, a riddle to solve, a challenge I adore,
Your eyes, a captivating labyrinth, where I yearn to explore.
Don't leave yet, my love, let the mystery unfold,
This intellectual connection, more precious than gold.
Like a scholar without a question, my mind would lose its quest,
If your presence faded, leaving an answer unguessed.
Your laughter, a melody of wit, that sets my thoughts ablaze,
Your touch, a whispered clue, guiding me through life's maze.
In the library of my life, you're the wisdom I seek,
Without you, my dear, my knowledge would be incomplete.
So stay with me, my love, and unravel with me hand in hand,
Let our love's journey forever explore this wonderland.
Together we'll seek the truth, a vibrant and endless quest,
Two souls entwined, forever learning, forever blessed.

A Melody Composed in Spring

A symphony of springtime, when you enter the scene,
A melody of hope, a love evergreen.
Your smile, a blooming flower, fragrant and ever so sweet,
Your eyes, a gentle breeze, where dreams and aspirations meet.
Don't leave yet, my love, let the springtime remain,
This renewal of our souls, a love that eases all pain.
Like a seed without sunshine, my dreams would lose their light,
If your presence faded, leaving an empty night.
Your laughter, a cascading waterfall, pure and ever bright,
Your touch, the gentle warmth of sun, chasing away the night.
In the garden of my life, you're the bloom I hold most dear,
Without you, my love, my happiness would disappear.
So stay with me, my love, and let the springtime unfold,
Let our love blossom, a story yet to be told.
Together we'll grow a love story, strong and true,
Two souls entwined, forever bathed in love's morning dew.

A Symphony of Rain

The world may weep in raindrops, a melancholic sound,
But with you, my love, a harmony can be found.
Your smile, a comforting ray, peeking through the clouds above,
Your eyes, a captivating ocean, reflecting endless love.
Don't leave yet, my love, let the rain gently fall,
This quiet symphony, a love that heals us all.
Like a wilting flower without nourishing rain,
If your presence faded, leaving only sorrow and pain.
Your laughter, a soothing melody, calming the storm within,
Your touch, a gentle whisper, washing away every sin.
In the grand orchestra of life, you're the calming refrain,
Without you, my dear, my music would be filled with strain.
So stay with me, my love, and listen to the rain's gentle song,
Let our love's symphony forever right every wrong.
Together we'll find solace, a melody soft and slow,
Two souls entwined, where love's warmth helps our spirits grow.

A Whisper Carried on Starlight

Words cannot reach the distance, where my heart longs to be,
But a whisper on starlight carries my love for thee.
Your smile, a distant galaxy, shimmering ever so bright,
Your eyes, a captivating nebula, where dreams take flight.
Don't leave yet, my love, let the starlight remain,
This celestial connection, a love that eases all pain.
Like a lost traveler without a guiding star,
If your presence faded, leaving me wandering afar.
Your laughter, a cosmic echo, filling the vast unknown,
Your touch, the gentle pull of gravity, drawing me ever home.
In the vast universe of life, you're the stardust I crave,
Without you, my dear, I'd be forever lost and enslaved.
So stay with me, my love, and let the starlight guide,
Let our love's whisper forever by your side confide.
Together we'll explore the cosmos, hand in hand, you and I,
Two souls entwined, beneath love's endless, starry sky.

A Haven in Your Voice

The world may shout its chaos, a noise I cannot bear,
But in your voice, my love, I find solace and prayer.
Your smile, the sweetest melody, a harmony so bright,
Your voice, a captivating verse, filling my world with light.
Don't leave yet, my love, let your voice always flow,
This calming symphony, a love that helps my spirit grow.
Like a lone bird without a song, my voice would lose its flight,
If your presence faded, leaving an empty night.
Your laughter, a vibrant chorus, lifting my spirit high,
Your words, a gentle comfort, drying every tear in my eye.
In the grand orchestra of life, you're the conductor's grace,
Without you, my dear, my music would lose its embrace.
So stay with me, my love, and sing a melody for me,
Let our love's symphony forever set our hearts free.
Together we'll create a joyous performance, vibrant and bold,
Two souls entwined, a love story forever to be told.

A Promise Whispered on the Wind

A promise whispered on the wind, a vow my heart holds dear,
To love you endlessly, my love, with every passing year.
Your smile, a whispered secret, on a gentle summer breeze,
Your eyes, a captivating story, that puts my heart at ease.
Don't leave yet, my love, let the promise take flight,
This unwavering connection, a love ever so bright.
Like a seed without fertile ground, my love would wither and
fade,
If your presence faded, leaving a love unmade.
Your laughter, a vibrant chorus, that sets my spirit free,
Your touch, a whispered promise, forever meant to be.
In the garden of my life, you're the bloom I adore,
Without you, my dear, my happiness would disappear.
So stay with me, my love, and let the promise unfold,
Let our love blossom, a story yet to be told.
Together we'll grow a love story, strong and true,
Two souls entwined, forever in love's embrace, me and you.

Captured in Your Gaze

Lost in a world of my own, adrift in thought's embrace,
Then your gaze meets mine, and time seems to find its place.
Your smile, a sunrise bursting, chasing away the night,
Your eyes, a captivating ocean, where stars forever shine bright.
Don't leave yet, my love, let me stay lost in your eyes,
A world of wonder unfolds, where every feeling thrives.
Like a star without the night sky, my light would lose its way,
If your presence faded, leaving an empty gray.
Your laughter, a cascading stream, pure and ever bright,
Your touch, a gentle anchor, holding me ever so tight.
In the vast expanse of life, you're the compass I crave,
Without you, my dear, I'd be forever lost and enslaved.
So stay with me, my love, let our gazes intertwine,
Let our love's story forever be a love truly divine.
Together we'll explore the depths of each other's soul,
Two souls entwined, where love makes us whole.

A Symphony of Silence

Words may stumble and falter, failing to express my heart,
But the silence between us speaks a love that sets us apart.
Your smile, a knowing glance, a secret we both hold dear,
Your eyes, a captivating mystery, where unspoken emotions appear.
Don't leave yet, my love, let the silence linger near,
This melody of connection, a love that conquers all fear.
Like a musician without a melody, my voice would be incomplete,
If your presence faded, leaving a love bittersweet.
Your laughter, a silent ripple, a joy that fills the air,
Your touch, a shared understanding, a love beyond compare.
In the grand orchestra of life, you're the harmony I seek,
Without you, my dear, my music would forever be meek.
So stay with me, my love, and let the silence unfold,
Let our love blossom, a story yet to be told.
Together we'll create a symphony, vibrant and profound,
Two souls entwined, in love's melody forever bound.

A Tapestry Woven with Dreams

Thread by thread, our dreams we weave, a tapestry so grand,
A masterpiece of aspirations, held ever close at hand.
Your smile, a vibrant thread of hope, adding joy to the design,
Your eyes, a depth of passion, where dreams and futures combine.
Don't leave yet, my love, let the dreams remain,
This tapestry of our journey, eases every pain.
Like a weaver without a loom, the threads would lose their hold,
If your presence faded, leaving a story untold.
Your laughter, a shimmering thread, woven with delight,
Your touch, a comforting thread, guiding me through the night.
In the grand design of life, you're the pattern I adore,
Without you, my dear, my dreams would forever be an empty chore.
So stay with me, my love, and let's weave hand in hand,
Let our love's tapestry forever withstand.
Together we'll create a masterpiece, vibrant and bold,
Two souls entwined, a future story to be told.

A Haven in Your Heart

The world may rage on, with storms and endless strife,
But within your heart, my love, I find solace in life.
Your smile, a calming sunset, painting the sky with ease,
Your heart, a tranquil ocean, bringing me inner peace.
Don't leave yet, my love, be my haven and guide,
A shelter from storms, where love can confide.
Like a lost ship without a harbor's embrace,
If your presence faded, leaving an empty space.
Your laughter, a soothing current, washing worries away,
Your touch, a safe harbor, where I can forever stay.
In the journey of life, you're the lighthouse I see,
Without you, my dear, I'd be lost at sea.
So stay with me, my love, let your heart be my guide,
Let our love be a fortress, forever by your side.
Together we'll face the storms, hand in hand, strong and true,
Two souls entwined, in love's everlasting hue.

A Whisper in the Library

Among towering shelves, where stories softly sleep,
A whispered word, a stolen glance, our connection runs deep.
Your smile, a worn book's inscription, a hidden treasure untold,
Your eyes, captivating chapters, with mysteries to unfold.
Don't leave yet, my love, let the silence ignite,
This spark of curiosity, a love burning ever so bright.
Like a scholar without a quest, my mind would lose its fire,
If your presence faded, leaving an unfulfilled desire.
Your laughter, a bookmark's gentle rustle, a joyful serenade,
Your touch, a whispered secret, on a forbidden page displayed.
In the library of my life, you're the knowledge I adore,
Without you, my dear, my world would be dull once more.
So stay with me, my love, and explore with me hand in hand,
Let our love's story be written, in this literary wonderland.
Together we'll turn every page, a vibrant and endless tale,
Two souls entwined, in a love story that will never fail.

A Melody Composed on a Rainy Day

The world may weep in raindrops, a melancholic sound,
But with you, my love, a vibrant melody can be found.
Your smile, a comforting ray, peeking through the clouds above,
Your voice, a captivating melody, a harmony of love.
Don't leave yet, my love, let the music play on,
This symphony of emotions, where sadness can't prolong.
Like a lone instrument without a song, my voice would be unheard,
If your presence faded, leaving a melody unstirred.
Your laughter, a soothing rhythm, chasing away the gloom,
Your touch, a gentle harmony, rewriting life's tune.
In the grand orchestra of life, you're the conductor I hold dear,
Without you, my dear, my music would be filled with fear.
So stay with me, my love, and compose with me in the rain,
Let our love's symphony forever ease away the pain.
Together we'll create a masterpiece, vibrant and bold,
Two souls entwined, a story forever to be told.

A Promise Carved in Stone

Etched in stone, like ancient lore, a promise set in time,
To love you with all my heart, a love that's truly thine.
Your smile, a timeless sculpture, beauty that will never fade,
Your eyes, a captivating wellspring, where dreams forever cascade.
Don't leave yet, my love, let the promise remain,
This unwavering connection, a love that eases all pain.
Like a forgotten monument without a story to tell,
If your presence faded, leaving an empty shell.
Your laughter, a timeless melody, echoing through the years,
Your touch, a gentle inscription, wiping away all tears.
In the grand tapestry of life, you're the thread I adore,
Without you, my dear, my world would be dull once more.
So stay with me, my love, and let the promise unfold,
Let our love blossom, a story yet to be told.
Together we'll build a monument, strong and true,
Two souls entwined, forever in love's embrace, me and you.

A Sanctuary in Your Smile

The world may be chaotic, a whirlwind of endless chase,
But in your smile, my love, I find a tranquil space.
Your smile, a calming meadow, where worries gently cease,
Your eyes, a captivating sunrise, bringing inner peace.
Don't leave yet, my love, let the sanctuary remain,
This haven of our connection, a love that eases all pain.
Like a weary traveler without a place to rest,
If your presence faded, leaving me forever distressed.
Your laughter, a calming stream, washing worries away,
Your touch, a safe harbor, where I can forever stay.
In the journey of life, you're the guiding light I see,
Without you, my dear, I'd be lost eternally.
So stay with me, my love, and let your smile always shine,
Let our love be a sanctuary, forever truly thine.
Together we'll face the world, hand in hand, strong and true,
Two souls entwined, in love's everlasting hue.

A Constellation of Laughter

Stars dance above, a celestial display,
But your laughter, my love, lights up a brighter way.
Your smile, a twinkling nova, exploding with pure delight,
Your eyes, a captivating galaxy, where laughter burns ever so bright.
Don't leave yet, my love, let the laughter ignite,
This cosmic connection, a love that chases away the night.
Like a lonely planet without a companion to share,
If your presence faded, leaving an emptiness to bear.
Your laughter, a shooting star's playful streak, a wish whispered free,
Your touch, the gentle pull of gravity, drawing me closer to thee.
In the vast universe of life, you're the stardust I crave,
Without you, my dear, my world would be a lonely, silent grave.
So stay with me, my love, let laughter be our guide,
Let our love's constellation forever brightly reside.
Together we'll explore the cosmos, hand in hand, you and I,
Two souls entwined, beneath love's laughter that paints the endless sky.

A Melody Composed at Dawn

The world awakens softly, with the first rays of light,
But your presence, my love, makes my whole world take flight.
Your smile, a gentle sunrise, painting the sky with gold,
Your voice, a captivating melody, a story yet untold.
Don't leave yet, my love, let the music begin,
This symphony of our souls, a love that eases all sin.
Like a songbird without a song to sing, my voice would lose its grace,
If your presence faded, leaving an empty space.
Your laughter, a vibrant chorus, awakening the day with glee,
Your touch, a whispered promise, forever meant to be.
In the grand orchestra of life, you're the composer I adore,
Without you, my dear, my music would forever be an empty roar.
So stay with me, my love, and sing a melody for me,
Let our love's symphony forever set our spirits free.
Together we'll create a masterpiece, vibrant and bold,
Two souls entwined, a love story forever to be told.

A Tapestry Woven with Time

Thread by thread, our moments we weave, a tapestry so grand,
A masterpiece of experiences, held ever close at hand.
Your smile, a vibrant thread of joy, adding warmth to the design,
Your eyes, a depth of shared memories, where love forever intertwine.
Don't leave yet, my love, let the tapestry grow,
This chronicle of our journey, a love that helps our spirits flow.
Like a loom without a weaver, the threads would lose their hold,
If your presence faded, leaving a story left untold.
Your laughter, a shimmering thread, woven with delight,
Your touch, a comforting thread, guiding me through the night.
In the grand design of life, you're the pattern I adore,
Without you, my dear, my memories would be dull once more.
So stay with me, my love, and let's weave hand in hand,
Let our love's tapestry forever withstand.
Together we'll create a masterpiece, vibrant and bold,
Two souls entwined, a tapestry of love's story to unfold.

A Spark Ignited in Your Eyes

A spark ignites within me, the moment you appear,
A captivating fire, a love both sweet and clear.
Your smile, a burning ember, glowing ever so bright,
Your eyes, a captivating furnace, where dreams take flight.
Don't leave yet, my love, let the flame flicker and grow,
This warmth of connection, a love that helps our spirits know.
Like a candle without a flame, my heart would lose its light,
If your presence faded, leaving an endless night.
Your laughter, a crackling fire, warming my soul with glee,
Your touch, a gentle ember, setting my spirit free.
In the journey of life, you're the spark I adore,
Without you, my dear, my world would be forever cold to the core.
So stay with me, my love, and let the fire ignite,
Let our love's flame forever burn ever so bright.
Together we'll face the darkness, hand in hand, strong and true,
Two souls entwined, in love's warmth, forever me and you.

A Whisper Carried on the Wind (A Playful Twist)

The wind whispers secrets, but this time it's a tease,
"Your crush is out there, go say hello, and put their heart at ease!"
Your smile, a playful breeze, ruffling leaves in delight,
Your eyes, a captivating ocean, sparkling ever so bright.
Don't be shy, my love, let the wind be your guide,
This chance encounter, a love that can't be denied.
Like a lone kite without a playful gust, your spirit would lose its flight,
If you hold back your feelings, leaving love in the fading light.
Your laughter, a contagious melody, filling the air with glee,
Your touch, a gentle nudge, a chance for you and me.
In the grand game of life, you're the player I adore,
Without you, my dear, my heart might forever be wanting more.
So take a leap, my love, let the wind carry you near,
Let our love story blossom, a future both happy and clear.
Together we'll create a joyful adventure, vibrant and bold,
Two souls entwined, a love story waiting to unfold.

A Melody Composed in Autumn

The leaves may change their colors, a season's gentle sway,
But with you, my love, beauty blossoms in a brand new way.
Your smile, a vibrant autumn leaf, painted with hues of gold,
Your eyes, a captivating forest, where secrets yet untold.
Don't leave yet, my love, let the colors remain,
This vibrant tapestry, a love that eases all pain.
Like a lone musician without a song for the changing year,
If your presence faded, leaving an empty, silent tear.
Your laughter, a cascading brook, a melody ever so bright,
Your touch, a gentle harvest, bringing warmth and delight.
In the grand orchestra of life, you're the changing symphony I
adore,
Without you, my dear, my world would be dull once more.
So stay with me, my love, and explore the changing scene,
Let our love's melody forever flourish and be evergreen.
Together we'll create a masterpiece, vibrant and bold,
Two souls entwined, a love story forever to be told.

A Promise Carved in Wood

Etched in the heartwood, a message strong and true,
To love you with all my being, a promise whispered to you.
Your smile, a growth ring of time, a story etched with care,
Your eyes, a captivating forest, where dreams and secrets share.
Don't leave yet, my love, let the promise take root,
This unwavering connection, a love that bears life's sweet fruit.
Like a forgotten sapling without sunlight's gentle kiss,
If your presence faded, leaving an emptiness I couldn't dismiss.
Your laughter, a rustling melody, leaves dancing in the breeze,
Your touch, a grounding root, giving my spirit ease.
In the grand garden of life, you're the bloom I adore,
Without you, my dear, my world would be dull once more.
So stay with me, my love, and let the promise unfold,
Let our love blossom, a story yet to be told.
Together we'll grow a love story, strong and true,
Two souls entwined, forever in love's embrace, me and you.

A Sanctuary in Your Spirit

The world may be a storm cloud, with troubles dark and vast,
But in your spirit, my love, I find serenity at last.
Your smile, a calming moonlight, guiding me through the night,
Your spirit, a captivating haven, where worries take flight.
Don't leave yet, my love, let the sanctuary remain,
This haven of our connection, a love that eases all pain.
Like a lost traveler without a compass to guide,
If your presence faded, leaving me forever to confide
Your laughter, a calming rain shower, washing worries away,
Your touch, a safe harbor, where I can forever stay.
In the journey of life, you're the guiding star I see,
Without you, my dear, I'd be lost eternally.
So stay with me, my love, and let your spirit always shine,
Let our love be a sanctuary, forever truly thine.
Together we'll face the storms, hand in hand, strong and true,
Two souls entwined, in love's everlasting hue.

A Symphony of Silence in a Crowded Room

The world may buzz and chatter, a symphony of sound,
But in the silence between us, a deeper love is found.
Your smile, a secret twinkle, in a sea of faces bright,
Your eyes, a captivating ocean, where stars forever ignite.
Don't leave yet, my love, let the quietude remain,
This unspoken understanding, a love that eases all strain.
Like a lone instrument without its melody's embrace,
If your presence faded, leaving an empty space.
Your laughter, a silent ripple, a joy that fills the air,
Your touch, a shared glance, a connection beyond compare.
In the grand orchestra of life, you're the harmony I seek,
Without you, my dear, my music would forever be meek.
So stay with me, my love, and let the silence unfold,
Let our love blossom, a story yet to be told.
Together we'll create a symphony, vibrant and profound,
Two souls entwined, in the hush where love's truest notes resound.

A Constellation of Memories

Stars dance above, a celestial display,
But the memories we create, light up a brighter way.
Your smile, a twinkling memory, forever etched in time,
Your eyes, a captivating nebula, where laughter and joy intertwine.
Don't leave yet, my love, let the memories ignite,
This cosmic connection, a love that burns ever so bright.
Like a lonely planet without a story to share,
If your presence faded, leaving an emptiness to bear.
Your laughter, a shooting star's playful streak, a wish we hold so dear,
Your touch, a gentle reminder, of moments we hold near.
In the vast universe of life, you're the stardust I adore,
Without you, my dear, my memories would be a lonely, silent chore.
So stay with me, my love, and let memories be our guide,
Let our love's constellation forever brightly reside.
Together we'll explore the cosmos of our shared past, you and I,
Two souls entwined, beneath love's tapestry that paints the endless sky.

A Melody Composed with Rainbows

The world may seem dull and gray, a canvas washed in rain,
But with you, my love, a vibrant rainbow paints the scene again.
Your smile, a spectrum of colors, a joyous burst of light,
Your eyes, a captivating kaleidoscope, where dreams take flight.
Don't leave yet, my love, let the colors remain,
This vibrant tapestry, a love that eases all pain.
Like a lone musician without a hopeful song,
If your presence faded, leaving an empty, mournful throng.
Your laughter, a vibrant melody, chasing away the gloom,
Your touch, a gentle harmony, rewriting life's tune.
In the grand orchestra of life, you're the conductor I hold dear,
Without you, my dear, my music would be filled with fear.
So stay with me, my love, and paint rainbows hand in hand,
Let our love's symphony forever color the land.
Together we'll create a masterpiece, vibrant and bold,
Two souls entwined, a story forever to be told.

A Spark Ignited in Your Voice

A spark ignites within me, the moment you start to speak,
A captivating melody, a love both gentle and meek.
Your smile, a warming ember, glowing with a gentle light,
Your voice, a captivating furnace, where dreams take flight.
Don't leave yet, my love, let the flame flicker and grow,
This warmth of connection, a love that helps our spirits flow.
Like a candle without a flame, my heart would lose its spark,
If your presence faded, leaving an empty, lonely dark.
Your laughter, a crackling fire, warming my soul with glee,
Your words, a gentle ember, setting my spirit free.
In the journey of life, you're the voice I adore,
Without you, my dear, my world would be forever silent to the core.
So stay with me, my love, and let the spark ignite,
Let our love's flame forever burn ever so bright.
Together we'll face the darkness, hand in hand, strong and true,
Two souls entwined, in love's warmth, forever me and you.

A Whisper Carried on Moonlight (A Bittersweet Tone)

Moonlight whispers secrets, a message soft and low,
"Your crush may feel the same, but fear keeps love from growing slow."
Your smile, a moonbeam's gentle touch, a fleeting, tender light,
Your eyes, a captivating mystery, hidden in the night.
Don't be discouraged, my love, let hope still softly gleam,
This spark of unspoken feelings, a love that's more than a dream.
Like a lone star without the moon's gentle grace,
If your feelings stay hidden, love might forever lose its place.
Your laughter, a melody unheard, a whisper on the breeze,
Your touch, a longing wish, carried on the shifting seas.
In the vast expanse of life, you're the distant star I adore,
Without you, my dear, my heart might ache forevermore.
So take a chance, my love, let the moonlight be your guide,
Share your whispered feelings, let love no longer hide.
Together you might create a love story, vibrant and bold,
Two souls entwined, beneath the moon's light, a love yet to unfold.

A Symphony Composed in the City

The city may roar and rumble, a symphony of sound,
But with you, my love, a melody of peace is found.
Your smile, a calming cafe's melody, a warm and inviting space,
Your eyes, a captivating bookstore, where stories find their place.
Don't leave yet, my love, let the music play on,
This urban symphony, a love that eases all the wrong.
Like a lone busker without a song to share,
If your presence faded, leaving an emptiness to bear.
Your laughter, a vibrant street performer, filling the air with glee,
Your touch, a gentle subway ride, taking me closer to thee.
In the grand orchestra of life, you're the composer I adore,
Without you, my dear, my world would be a monotonous chore.
So stay with me, my love, and explore the city's embrace,
Let our love's symphony forever find its rightful place.
Together we'll create a vibrant rhythm, strong and true,
Two souls entwined, in love's melody, forever me and you.

A Tapestry Woven with Dreams (A Playful Approach)

Thread by thread, our silly jokes we weave, a tapestry so grand,
A masterpiece of laughter, held ever close at hand.
Your smile, a vibrant thread of joy, adding mischief to the design,
Your eyes, a captivating wellspring, where dreams and silliness combine.
Don't leave yet, my love, let the laughter unfold,
This tapestry of our connection, a love that's brave and bold.
Like a loom without a playful weaver, the threads would lose their hold,
If your presence faded, leaving a story left untold.
Your laughter, a shimmering thread, woven with delight,
Your touch, a playful nudge, keeping our spirits light.
In the grand design of life, you're the partner I adore,
Without you, my dear, my jokes would forever be a dull bore.
So stay with me, my love, and let's weave hand in hand,
Let our love's tapestry be filled with laughter in every strand.
Together we'll create a masterpiece, vibrant and bold,
Two souls entwined, in a love story that's forever joyful and unfolds.

A Spark Ignited in Your Passion

A spark ignites within me, the moment you chase a dream,
A captivating fire, a love that's both fierce and keen.
Your smile, a burning ember, glowing with ambition's might,
Your eyes, a captivating furnace, where passions take flight.
Don't leave yet, my love, let the flame flicker and grow,
This warmth of inspiration, a love that helps our spirits flow.
Like a candle without a purpose, my heart would lose its spark,
If your presence faded, leaving an empty, lonely dark.
Your laughter, a crackling fire, warming my soul with glee,
Your touch, a gentle ember, setting my spirit free.
In the journey of life, you're the flame I adore,
Without you, my dear, my world would be forever stagnant to the core.
So stay with me, my love, and let the fire ignite,
Let our love's flame forever burn ever so bright.

About the Author

Mrigendra Bharti, born on June 29, 2004, in South Delhi, India, is a multifaceted individual recognized as the owner of Mrigendra Bharti Group InfoTech India Co. Pvt Ltd. Beyond his entrepreneurial endeavors, he is a distinguished music producer, director, and a budding writer.

Embarking on his professional journey at a young age, Mrigendra Bharti's visionary leadership has led to the establishment of several successful ventures, including Croma Music Series Entertainment, Sellbrochure, Fauget Innovative, and more.

What sets Mrigendra apart is his early initiation into the world of business. His foray into the unknown realms of entrepreneurship began during his 10th-grade years, where he delved into the music industry. This initial venture laid the foundation for subsequent achievements, showcasing his dedication and resilience.

Having honed his skills in music, Mrigendra Bharti not only demonstrated significant growth in his craft but also expanded his professional network. His passion extends beyond music, encompassing app and website development, as well as graphic design.

Fueled by his creative aspirations, Mrigendra established the Mrigendra Bharti Group, a company specializing in website and app development. Currently, he collaborates with a dedicated team, collectively working on ambitious projects that promise innovation and excellence.

Mrigendra's journey serves as an inspiration, particularly for today's students, highlighting the potential of youthful determination and the ability to transform innovative ideas into successful businesses. As he continues to make strides in various domains, Mrigendra Bharti remains a dynamic force, contributing vibrancy to the realms of business, music, and technology.

Read more at https://www.imwriter-mrigendra.rf.gd.